AMAZON ECHO SHOW 8 USER MANUAL

A Complete Step by Step User Guide to Master Your Amazon Echo Show 8; Including Advance Tips, Tricks for Alexa Skills and Essential Device Set-ups

BY

JOEY COLLINS

Table of content

Introduction

This book is a follow up on the previous book which covers the Amazon Echo Show 5. As you would expect, Amazon released an alternative echo show device: the **Amazon Echo Show 8**. This latest echo show device is an upgrade of the echo show 5 and it's packed full with many exciting features.

As with the echo show 5, I have dissected the Amazon Echo Show 8 in this user manual. If you have got yourself this device, I say a big congratulation to you; you are in for a treat! This beginner's manual to echo show 8 will help you understand your device so as to maximize its use. I have taking time to explore the echo show 8, and in the chapters of this book you will find simple step by step instruction to help you gain full mastery of the echo show 8.

The preliminary part of this manual briefly explains specifications of the Echo Show 8. This lets you get conversant with what the Echo Show 8 looks like and have an idea of what it can do. The first chapter explains how to set up your device for first-time use. All the steps you need to take are explained in detail. The second chapter continues from the first, covering more set up procedures and helping you get started with the device. It is in this chapter that you will learn how to personalize your device by adding your pictures, and other personal settings.

The third chapter explains Alexa features such as routines, blueprints, and all other necessary Alexa skills.

Chapter 4 focuses on helping you enjoy the best sound experience with your Echo Show 8. You are taught how to listen to podcasts, online radio, and find music from your Echo Show 8. The next chapter, Chapter 5 will teach you how to use your Echo Show 8 with other smart home devices and enjoy the power of Alexa as a smart home hub.

Chapter 6 focuses on how to make video calls using the popular Drop In feature. You also have several tips on how to protect your privacy in this chapter. For those with kids, this chapter will teach you how to protect them from explicit content and have only materials that are age appropriate for them. Chapter Seven explains how you can keep in touch while using your Echo Show 8. How do you make phone calls, and send messages with your Echo Show 8? You learn all about that in Chapter 7.

Chapter 8 teaches you how you can make purchases safely with Alexa. You will learn how to set up passwords and how to order products by speaking to Alexa. In the next chapter, Chapter 9, you will learn how to use IFTTT recipes and Alexa skills with your Echo Show 8.

In the course of using the Echo Show 8, you may encounter a few issues. The final chapter deals with possible challenges that may pop up and how you can fix such challenges. It is in this chapter that you will learn how to effectively troubleshoot your device and get it working fine again.

In all, this manual is written in a way that you have an in-depth and overall understanding of the Echo Show 8, such that you will be able to use it and enjoy all it is capable of doing. Now go ahead and enjoy the awesomeness of the Echo Show 8.

What's New in the Echo Show 8?

The Echo Show 8 is one of three Alexa powered Echo Show devices. There is the Echo Show 5, the Echo Show and the Echo Show 8. All three share very similar designs with similar features although have different sizes and prices. The Echo Show 8 packs a lot of features for its price being something of a midpoint between the Echo Show 5 and the Echo Show. The Echo Show 8 comes in a wedge shape with a fabric back. You can choose between two colors; white and black.

The Echo Show 8 has an 8-inch screen that automatically adjusts its brightness depending on room lighting. The screen is good enough to let you see from a good distance without holding it. The display is good for displaying photos. As for sound, dual 2-inch speakers and a bass port pump out 10 watts of sound power.

With the Echo Show 8, you have a variety of video platforms to entertain yourself with. You can view videos from Hulu, Amazon Prime Video, and NBC. Music is available from Amazon Music, Spotify, Pandora and Apple Music. You will also enjoy video calls to other Echo Show Devices with the 1-megapixel camera and the two far-field microphones. With those microphones, your device will hear you loud and clear even when you are not with the device. You can protect your privacy by shutting off the camera using the camera shutter.

CHAPTER 1

Setting Up Your Device For First Time Use

Now that you have purchased your Echo show device how do you set it up? To set up your Echo show device is not as difficult as it appears. All you need to do is to follow these steps. Before then, you will need the following a laptop or a PC, a tablet, a smartphone, and an internet connection. You'll also need to have an Amazon Prime subscription. Now here's what to do.

1. Download the Alexa app. You can get to the app from the Google Play store Amazon app store or on alexa.com.
2. Plugin your Echo show 8 to a power source and put it on.

3. If it is on the device respond by saying “Hello” your Echo device is ready to set up.
4. The device will ask you to select your preferred language. Afterward, it will ask you to connect to the internet. Connect to the Wi-Fi and login to your Amazon Prime account. Read and agree to the terms and conditions you will be presented with.
5. Go to Amazon.com/code and register your device. When you register, you will obtain a code with which you will use to continue your Echo Show 8 set up.
6. When setting up your device, an update may be available. If an update is available, you will be notified. Choose **install now** so

that the updates will be installed. It will take some time, wait until the update is complete.

7. Once the update is complete, you can continue your setup process. A brief video will be shown to introduce you to the features of your Echo Show 8. You are advised to watch the video.

Pairing Your Smartphone with your Echo Show 8

Your Echo Show 8 can also play music from your smartphone like regular Bluetooth speakers. The Echo Show 8 is Bluetooth enabled like it's predecessor. With it, you can stream music, podcasts, play audio from your smartphone or other Bluetooth devices. With its twin two-inch speakers, the Echo Show 8 gives out superior quality sound. Hence you will enjoy your music a lot much more by playing it through your Echo Show 8 device.

Here is how to pair your device with your smartphone.

1. Turn on the Bluetooth option on your smartphone.
2. Set your Bluetooth option to "Pair". Also, make sure your smartphone and the Echo Show 8 are not far apart.
3. Ensure your Echo device is ready and then say the word **Pair**. Alexa will pick up the command to pair and get into pairing mode.
4. Go to the Bluetooth option on your smartphone. You will see a list of visible devices. Select the Echo Show 8. The devices will connect.

Sometimes a passkey will automatically be generated.

5. Alexa will let you know if the connection is successful or not.

Now that you have connected your device with your smartphone, you can disconnect at any time. Tell Alexa to disconnect by saying "Disconnect" and the connection will be terminated. Alexa will notify when it is done. Once paired, you can always connect your smartphone by saying "Alexa Connect". Your Echo Show 8 will immediately connect to your smartphone.

Setting Up Alexa Voice Profiles on Your Echo Show 8

There's a special Alexa skill that allows you to easily get voice profiles in place and then get Alexa to recognize your voice. This feature allows you to teach Alexa to recognize your voice and act on your instructions. This feature also allows Alexa to differentiate between the voices of multiple users. You can set up the voice profile feature in two different ways. You can set it up either through your Echo Show 8 or via Alexa on your smartphone, or tablet.

To do this using the Alexa app on your smartphone or tablet, take these steps.

1. Launch the Alexa app on your smartphone or tablet.
2. Sign in to your Amazon account. Ensure you sign in to the account that is linked to the Echo device you wish to train to recognize your voice.
3. Follow this path **Menu** > **Settings** > **Account Settings**.

4. Select "**Recognized Voices**"
5. You'd notice where "**Create a Voice Profile"** is written. Click on the **+** sign beside it.
6. A disclaimer will pop up. Read the disclaimer and select "**Continue"**.
7. Do as the voice prompts say. Say what the voice prompts ask you to say. You may have to repeat a few words to ensure that your voice is correctly captured. While carrying this activity, ensure that you are in a quiet space free of background noise and disturbance. It helps to keep the Echo Show 8 about 12 to 17 feet away from walls to prevent echoes.
8. Tap "**Try again**" after each repetition to get better results. This trains Alexa better. Once you

have completed the process, select "**Done**".

With these steps, you have successfully taught Alexa to recognize your voice. From start to finish, it takes a little less than 20 minutes to get this done. Patience and pronouncing the words properly is key. In the end, you have a voice profile which means that Alexa can identify you as a person.

To set up an Alexa voice profile from the Echo Show 8 device is equally as simple as the preceding process.

1. Speak out loud and say "Alexa learn my voice"
2. Alexa will mention Amazon profiles registered to it. If the profiles mentioned are not yours, respond by saying "no".

3. Say "yes" when your profile is mentioned.
4. Alexa will ask you to say some phrases after it. Repeat these phrases properly.
5. With that, Alexa has learned to recognize you from your voice.

You can test your device to see if it can recognize your voice. It is easy. Simply ask Alexa "Who am I?" Alexa will tell you who you are based on the profile you registered on it. If it gets the profile correctly, the process has been successful.

How to Delete Your Alexa Voice Profile

Chances are that you may wish to delete a voice profile you have set up for one reason or the other. Most times when your device fails to recognize your voice you may have to delete the profile and create another profile. Whatever your reason may be, it is possible to delete your profile and it is not a difficult process.

You can follow this procedure on the Alexa app.

1. Go to the "**Settings**" menu.
2. Go to "**Alexa Account".**
3. Choose "**Recognized voices**". There will be a "**Delete my Voice**" option. If you do not see it, look out for an "**Automatically Recognize Voices**" option. If it's on, turn it off. Once you turn this off you can create a new voice profile.

Helping Alexa Recognize New Voices

You can allow Alexa to recognize other people and do what they ask it to. You will have to add the person as a new user. To do this, you will install Alexa on that person's device. Pair the person's device and tap on "**Add New User**" and follow the setup instructions. After adding the person as a user, go to the **"Settings Menu"** and select "**Your Voice"** to create a new voice profile.

With this, not only will be able to speak to your device and get a response, other members of your family will be able to have a great experience with the device in a personal manner.

Listen to More Phrases

Alexa listens to all the comments you give her. The more you speak to your device, the more Alexa learns and adds more phrases to her system. With time you will grow to speak more than just basic commands with Alexa. To listen to music from Amazon, you can ask it by saying "Alexa, play Chris Brown". If you want to pause the music you can say "Alexa Stop music"

Setting Up Amazon Household

Amazon Household is an amazing feature that allows you to share subscriptions to Amazon content with members of your household. To create an Amazon Household profile;

1. Open your account.

2. Go to "**Amazon Household**" in your account.
3. Tap on "**Add Teen**" or "**Add an Adult**" to send an email invite. Enter the invited person's details. The recipients must accept the invitation for the process to continue. For teens, accepting the invitation ends the process.
4. For adults, you must enter the name and email address of the invited adult.
5. If you want to share his Amazon benefits like prime with the invited person, select the "**Share**" option.
6. Confirm the name and email address of the person you wish to invite. Select "**Send Invite**". The person has 2 weeks to accept the invitation. If the person doesn't

accept within 2 weeks, the invitation is revoked.

Adding a child to Amazon Household is equally easy too. Follow the process as though you were adding an adult or teenager. However, click on "**Add a Child**".

Turning Amazon FreeTime On and Off

The Amazon Alexa app can be used to set up and run the Amazon FreeTime service. With the Alexa app, the FreeTime service can be set up to work on your Echo Show 8 and other Kindle devices.

FreeTime gives your children access to thousands of content classified according to age and educational levels. There are several educational songs, games, and videos available that not just teach but entertain. If you're a parent you can set limits to the content your child is exposed to on FreeTime. You can set time limits and other limits.

To turn off Amazon FreeTime;

1. Launch the Alexa app
2. Select the Echo device
3. Tap on "**FreeTime**" and switch it off.

Using Voice Control While Offline

The Echo Show 8 can work without being connected to the internet. That is, you can speak to it and it will respond even when it is not connected to the internet. This is possible to a feature known as Local Voice control.

Because it is not connected to the internet, local voice control supports limited requests. You can only turn on lights, set and stop alarms, control volume on your device and other offline tasks. Here's how to manage local voice control Settings.

1. Select the "**Devices**" icon.
2. Ensure your device is connected and compatible with the smart home hub.
3. Select the "**Local Voice Control**" option and switch it on or off.

CHAPTER 2

Creating a Custom Home Screen on Your Echo Show 8

It is usual for users to want to tune their device to reflect their taste and personality as much as is possible. Many users do not find the pre-set home screen images captivating enough. Hence, there is a strong urge to change the images to relatable or personal images. You can upload images for your home screen through Alexa. Follow these steps for a custom home screen.

1. Drag down the top panel by swiping from top to bottom of your Echo Show 8.
2. Select "settings" and then choose "**Home and Clock**"
3. Tap "**Clock**"

4. You'd see available images from which you can choose a new home screen image.

To add new photos from your smartphone to your Echo device do the following

1. Launch the Alexa app
2. Go to the "**Devices**" tab on the drop-down menu.
3. Select the Alexa device you wish to personalize.
4. Scroll through the settings. When you get to "**Home Screen Background**" stop and select it.
5. A list of photos from your smartphone will dropdown.
6. Choose your preferred image

Setting up Night Mode

When all the info is displayed at full-screen brightness all day and all night, your battery takes a toll. This will mean you will have to charge your device now and then. This will hamper long term use. To save power and keep charging times farther apart, you can enable the night mode feature.

The night mode feature dims the screen at night. It will also let you know when it should be turned off or on. The night mode is also good for your eyesight as it protects your eyes from bright screen lights at night.

To manage the Night Mode feature,

1. Go to “**Settings**”
2. Click on “**Home and Clock**”
3. Select "**Night Mode**" and turn on "**Night Time Clock**"

Adding Facebook Photos to your Echo Show 8 Home Screen

You are free to add your Facebook pictures to your Echo Show 8 home screen. The pictures will come in the form of a slideshow. It works by linking your Facebook account to your Amazon account. Here's how to go about this

1. Put all the photos you want in the slideshow into a single album on Facebook.
2. Once you have created the album, set the privacy settings to public
3. Open the Amazon app on your Smartphone.
4. Move down to "**Settings**" and then choose "**Photos**"
5. Select "**Link Account**" and then log in to your Facebook account to link both accounts.

6. Go to your Echo Show 8 and open the "**Settings**" menu.
7. Follow this path **Home Screen** > **Background** > **Facebook**
8. All the albums from Facebook will be displayed. Select an album and click the back button.
9. Go to settings and select on the "**Home Icon**"
10. With these, your selected album photos will be displayed on your home screen. You can also specifically as for your album photos by asking for them. You can say "Alexa, show me my album photos"

Adding Photos from Amazon Prime on your Home Screen

While Facebook photos on your home screen can work in every country, some countries and regions in the world do not support Amazon Prime photos. If Amazon Prime works in your country, then you can enjoy a great experience with the prime photos plug-in.

The procedure for adding Amazon Prime photos is very similar to the procedure for adding Facebook photos. Follow these steps to get it done.

1. Open **Amazon Photos** on your smartphone.
2. Tap on the three dots icon that is on the upper right corner.
3. Scroll to "**Create Album**" on the menu that pops up and then give the album a name.

4. Choose the photos you wish to include in the album and then select "**Create**"
5. On your Echo Show 8, go to "**Settings**" tap on "**Display**" and then select "**Background**".
6. Select Prime Photos when you see it.
7. Choose the album you just created and select the "**Home Icon**".
8. The photos in the Amazon Prime Photos album will be displayed. You can, on the alternative, ask Alexa to display your Prime Photos album.

Taking Selfies on your Echo Show 8

Your Echo Show 8 has a 1mp front camera that can take selfies. You just simply request Alexa to take a picture for her to take a picture. You can say "Alexa, take a picture" and the picture is taken.

All photos taken will be automatically saved on your Amazon account. Alexa will ask you to select what type of photograph you'd want. Options available will be a single shot, a burst (which are four shots taken a minute apart), and sticker mode.

Viewing Your Photos on your device

The process of enjoying your photos on the Echo Show 8 is not complicated at all. Saying "Show my photos" allows you to view your stored photographs on Amazon prime. You can view slideshows by doing this

1. Swipe in a top-down pattern.
2. Select Settings on the top right corner of the screen.

3. Follow this path **Display** > **Photo Slideshow.**
4. Your slideshows will be displayed on the Echo Show 8. You can adjust the speed with which the images change from the "**Slideshow speed**" option.

Deleting your photos

You can delete your photos as easily as you add them. Just go to the Amazon prime photos app and delete the photos you wish to delete. Here is how to delete the photos.

1. Select the Prime Photos app on your smartphone and launch it.
2. Choose the "**Albums**" option at the bottom left and then choose "**Photo Booth**".

3. Select the picture or pictures you wish to delete
4. Click on the three dots in the top right corner.
5. Tap on the "**More**" button.
6. Select "**Delete**". The selected pictures will be moved to trash.
7. Click on the three dots on the upper right corner.
8. Tap on the "**More**" button.
9. Select "**Delete**". The pictures will be moved to trash.

Setting Up Minimal Home Screen Backgrounds

With your Echo Show 8, you can choose the option of creating a minimal home screen background. If you don't want any pictures displayed on the home screen background, this is the option for you. It's done this way

1. Go to the "**Settings Option**"
2. Thereafter, go to "**Display**"
3. Select "**Theme**"
4. Choose "**Minimal**".
5. Your default home screen background will be set to minimal display.

CHAPTER 3

How to Set Up Routines

You can give Alexa individual instructions but with time it's going to be a bore. You can set up a routine that does all the things you give individual instructions for. You can have a routine that turns on the lights; make coffee, and plays music with one command.

In older versions, Alexa could only carry out a single instruction at a time. With the new routines settings, a single command can result in several actions.

Here's how to create routines that work

1. Launch the Alexa app on your smartphone.
2. Choose the "**Menu**" icon top left corner on the screen.
3. Select "**Routines**"

4. Select the **+** icon in the upper right corner. This will unfold a new tab.
5. Choose "**Create Routine**"
6. Select "**When This Happens**" and choose an appropriate trigger.

When you have done these, options like Voice, Schedule, Device, Location, Alarm and Echo Button will appear. When you select a trigger, e.g. Echo Button, it means that once you push the Echo Button, it will carry out the activities lined up and tied to the routines.

If it is Voice you choose as a trigger, your Voice will be the trigger to start or end the routine. You can begin your routine with "Alexa, I'm awake", or "Alexa, I'm going to sleep".

Setting Device as the trigger lets you begin the routine by Alexa. When you set Alarm as your trigger, your routine will start as soon as you dismiss an alarm. When you select Location as a trigger, the routine will start as soon as you arrive at a particular location.

1. Select "**Add Action**" and add every task you want to be carried out on the routine. These tasks may include switching on the lights, playing music, etc.
2. Select "**Save**". Based on your trigger, your routine is ready to go.

Set Up Scheduled Routines

You can set routines that start and end at certain times by themselves. Here's how you set these up.

1. Start the Alexa app and select the "**Menu**" in the top right corner of the screen.
2. Choose the option "**Routines**".
3. Choose the **+** icon
4. Select the following options following this path **When This Happens** > **Schedule** > **Time**
5. Choose the precise time you want the schedule to begin.
6. Select **OK**
7. If you wish the schedule to repeat at certain times choose "**Repeat**".
8. Select the days of the week you want the schedule to go off and then click "**Done**".

Working With Alexa Blueprints

If you didn't know, Alexa Blueprints allows Echo Show owners to create customized skills and responses without any need to learn to code. With Alexa Blueprints, you can develop an Alexa skill and get it approved all within minutes.

It is very much like developing an app only in this case, there is no code involved. You can publish these skills and share them with others online at the Alexa Skills store. These skills function like apps on your Echo Show 8.

Blueprints can help you create skills that are fun and helpful to you and other Amazon users. Blueprints take in data you provide it like family, work, routine, etc and use templates to come up with great skills. Some blueprints include Trivia, personal trainer and others like it.

Creating a Blueprint is easy.

1. Use your Amazon account to sign in at Blueprints on the website which is Blueprints.amazon.com
2. Select a template you'd like to use.
3. After selecting your template, read up on the template description. It will give you clues on how best to create the skill you have in mind.
4. Select the "**Make your own**" option to begin building your skill.
5. Delete and fill in the details as you would wish. There are several fields to be filled.
6. Select a name for your skill. Choose a name that best describes it.
7. Wait for a few minutes. Your skill will be ready for use shortly.
8. You can then launch the skill and start making interactions with it. If

you'd like others to use your skill too, you can publish the skill. Go to "**Skills You Have Made**" and then click on "**Details**". Afterward, select "**Share with others**"

9. Publish your skill by selecting "**Publish to Skills Store**", and then select "**Skills you Have Made**".
10. Type in the name you use on Alexa Skills Store.
11. A fresh tab will be launched. Select the category your skill falls into. While making your selection, use the right keywords that let people find your skill easily.
12. Fill out the policy forms while properly filling the target audience.

13. Go through the information you have supplied and ensure they are correct.
14. Submit the information and await review.
15. You will receive an email stating whether the skill has been accepted or rejected.

Alexa Guard

Alexa Guard helps out in periods of emergency. The feature helps you keep an eye on things at home whenever you are away. The feature works on cooperation with your security feature letting you remain in charge.

The feature allows the Echo Show 8 to ensure you are aware of any potential threat. It makes use of the microphones to listen to fire alarms or any other alarms in your home. It is like your dependable housekeeper who keeps an eye on your home whenever you're away. To enable Alexa Guard;

1. Start the Alexa app on your phone.
2. Click the three-dot icon.
3. Select "**Settings**"
4. Scroll down the list and choose "**Guard**"
5. Put in and confirm your address and zip code. Once it is confirmed, features like Away Lighting mode, carbon monoxide detection, and breaking glass detection will be enabled.
6. You enable Alexa Guard by saying "**Alexa, I'm leaving**". To disable it you say "**Alexa, I'm home**".

Once this feature is enabled, alarms, when detected, will trigger Alexa to send you a notification in audio clips.

Alexa Hunches

Alexa Hunches notifies you if any of your smart home devices is out of place. It detects anything that is not in order and attempts to fix it. You may have forgotten to turn off the light and have said goodnight to Alexa, she may notify you of the lights that are still on.

Another Hunch could be when you say goodnight to Alexa with a playlist still on. Alexa will remind you that the playlist is still on. You can choose to accept a hunch by saying "**Yes**" or decline by saying "**No**".

To switch off Alexa Hunches, you can simply say "**Disable Hunches**". Saying "**Enable Hunches**" turns the feature on.

You can also go to the Alexa app to turn it on and off.

CHAPTER 4

How to Set Up Multi-Room Music

Multi-Room is a special feature that lets you stream music on your Echo devices throughout the home. This means you can stream a particular song or playlist and all Echo devices in your home will play the music at the same time. This synchronized music streaming is a great feature and lets you listen to the same song as you walk through your home.

For Multi-Room to work, all the devices must be on the same Wi-Fi network. You will also be required to possess an account with Amazon Prime or Amazon Music Unlimited. When you are playing with Amazon Prime, you can play one music stream on all devices. With Amazon

Music Unlimited, you will be able to play several music streams on your Echo Devices at the same time. What you need to do is outlined below.

1. Start the Alexa app from your phone
2. Visit the **Smart Home Control** tab and open it
3. Click on the **+** sign
4. Select "**Add Multi-Room Music Speakers**"
5. You can now start a new group by giving it a name and grouping all your Echo devices together under it.
6. Choose the devices you want to add and click on "**Save**"
7. Once the group is set, whatever you stream will be streamed on all

the devices that you added to the Multi-Room group.

You can play, pause or skip the music from any device in the Multi-Room group. You can be in the living room and skip the music right there and it will work.

Listening to Music

Playing and enjoying music from your Echo Show 8 is something very simple. You can request your device to play music by simply saying "Alexa, play music". You can even request for particular artists or songs. Alexa users have access to millions of songs when they have Amazon Prime memberships and Amazon Music Unlimited memberships.

Streaming Playlists with Alexa Voice Command

It gets better with each device. With your Echo Show 8 device, you can stream playlists. You can give the voice command through your smartphone or you can ask Alexa directly by asking the device.

Streaming Music via Bluetooth

You can stream music from your Echo Show 8 using a Bluetooth Speaker. While Multi-Room Music does not work over Bluetooth, you can stream music over Bluetooth using Bluetooth speakers. To stream music over Bluetooth;

1. Keep your Echo Show Device not far from your Bluetooth speaker.

2. Turn on your Bluetooth speaker and turn on its Bluetooth
3. Go to the Pairing function and keep it on
4. Launch the Alexa app on your Echo Show device
5. Choose the option "**Devices**"
6. Select your device
7. Select "**Bluetooth Devices**"
8. Click on the option "**Pair a New Device**" when it appears
9. A list bearing available devices will appear. Choose the Bluetooth speaker once you see it.
10. Connect to it
11. Say, "**Alexa, play music**" to begin playing music from the Bluetooth speaker.

Listening to Podcasts on Amazon Echo Show 5

You have to several hundreds of podcasts. Alexa can get you any podcast available on Amazon. To get this feature, ask Alexa to play any particular podcast for you. The user experience has been praised for its simplicity and quality.

Listening to Podcasts without Adding Skills

By default, Alexa plays the podcasts you listen to via skills such as TuneIn, Stitcher, and AnyPod. If for instance, you ask Alexa to play a podcast, it will play it from any of those podcast services. Your podcast will continue only if you do not switch to another podcast provider. If that occurs, you will have to start afresh. The steps to playing podcasts via Alexa are given

1. Start the Alexa app on your phone.
2. Go to the main menu.
3. Select "**Music, Video & Books**"
4. A drop-down menu will be displayed, choose the "**TuneIn**" option.
5. Tap on "**Podcasts**".
6. Browse through the podcasts available and select your preference.
7. Select the speaker you would want to play the podcast through.

Making Podcasts Play in Alexa as Part of Routine

We saw earlier what routines are and what they do. The good news is that you can add podcasts to your routine. So when the routine is triggered the podcast will play as part of the tasks outlined for that routine. To add podcasts to any routine;

1. Start the Alexa app.
2. Go to the menu option at the top left corner of the screen and tap on it.
3. Select the "**Routines**" option.
4. Select **+** icon
5. Choose the "**When this Happens**" option.

6. Select a trigger for your routine. You can choose Voice, Schedule or any other trigger displayed on the screen.
7. Type in the phrase you wish to use if you choose the voice option.
8. Tap the save button
9. Choose "**Add Action +**".
10. Select "**Music**"
11. Choose the music provider in this case "**TuneIn**"
12. Type in the title of the podcast you wish to add.
13. Click "**Add**"
14. Click "**Add Again**"
15. Click "**Create**"
16. With these, anytime the trigger you have set is activated, your Alexa powered Echo Show 8 will play your favorite podcast.

Podcast Playback in Alexa with AnyPod

AnyPod as an Alexa skill offers a more enjoyable listening experience on Echo Show devices than other podcast services. The sounds on Anypod are also clearer and crisper. With AnyPod, you can subscribe to a podcast, you have more playback options and can play the previous episodes without any problems whatsoever.

You can activate this skill by simply saying "**Alexa, enable the AnyPod skill**". You can also do it yourself by going through these steps.

1. Start the Alexa app
2. Choose "**Menu**", in the upper left corner of the screen.

3. Select the option "**Skills**" from the options that will dropdown.
4. There will be a search bar, type in "**AnyPod**" and push the search button.
5. Once you see AnyPod in the results, tap and activate.
6. With this, you can play your favorite AnyPod podcasts from your Echo Show 8.

Streaming Podcasts via Bluetooth

It is possible to stream podcasts from a Bluetooth enabled device that would be paired with your Echo Show 8. First of all, pair the mobile device with your Echo Show, and then search for and play the podcast you wish to play. You can check the first chapter of this manual for a guide on how to pair your smartphone and your Echo Show device.

Listening to Audiobooks

Alexa can play kindle audiobooks, so if you have any audiobooks on Kindle, and want to listen to them, Alexa can play them for you. Simply say "**Alexa read {mention audiobook title}**". Playback control is also easy, say "Pause" if you want Alexa to pause reading.

Listening to the Radio with Alexa

If you love to listen to the radio for special content, you have nothing to fear. With Alexa, you will not miss those special broadcasts, sports, reports, and news. You can easily listen to the radio on your Echo Show by following steps;

1. Start the Alexa app.
2. Click on the icon with three lines.
3. Click on "**Skills**".
4. Click on the categories button
5. Select "**Music, Audio and News**"
6. There will be several radio stations like MyTuner, Radio Paradise, Simple Radio
7. Choose the one you wish to listen to
8. Subsequently, you can ask Alexa to play any channel from any skill. For example, "Alexa, ask Radio Paradise to play BBC"

Watching YouTube and Netflix Videos

You can watch YouTube videos on your Echo Show device but you will have to go through a browser. This is because there is no skill for YouTube. You cannot ask Alexa to open YouTube and search for a video.

For Netflix videos, you cannot access content from Netflix on your Echo Show device because Netflix supports portrait viewing and your Echo Show Device does not.

Watching Amazon Prime Video

Amazon Prime provides access to thousands of videos via Amazon Prime Videos. With an Amazon Prime account, you can view videos on your Echo Show 8. You can stream the videos available online and the videos on your Amazon Prime Library. Once your network is stable, the experience is awesome.

Simply ask Alexa "Alexa, show me my video library" or "Show me TV shows"

Skyping with the Echo Show 8

You can make and answer Skype calls with your Echo Show device. This is a feature you can activate by speaking to Alexa. You will have to note these before you start making skype calls;

1. Your device must be up to date with the latest version of the Alexa app.
2. Open the Alexa app and link your Skype account with your Amazon account.
3. Enable the option to allow Alexa Communications in the Alexa app.

Here is how to go about linking your Skype account to Alexa;

1. Launch the Alexa app and tap on Menu
2. Select "**Settings**"
3. Next, click on "**Communications**"
4. Choose "**Skype**"
5. Sign in to your skype account and follow the instructions provided on linking your Skype account with Alexa.

Once your Skype account is linked with Alexa, you can call anyone on Skype by saying to Alexa, "**Alexa, Skype {Mention the contact's name}**". Whenever a Skype comes through, you can answer it by telling Alexa "Alexa, answer". Skype calls on Alexa are great and the quality is great as well.

CHAPTER 5

Setting up Smart Home Devices

As improvements have been made to make Alexa smarter and better, Alexa can work in concert with several smart devices in your home and lets you control them from your Echo Show 8.

Today the Alexa AI has been able to sync up and work seamlessly with smart devices to make your home more comfortable. In this chapter, we'll look at how to set up a smart home hub with your Echo Show device.

1. Before you sync any smart home devices e.g. lights, cameras, coffee makers, etc. Ensure that they are set up and functional.

2. Also, make sure that your Smart home devices are compatible with Alexa and your Echo Show 8.
3. Follow the manufacturer's guide on Setting up the smart home devices in your home.
4. If your device software is not up to date, download and install the currently available updates.
5. Now connect all the devices to the Wi-Fi connection your Echo Show 8 is connected to.

These steps outlined above do not automatically connect your smart devices and make your Echo Show 8 a smart home devices hub. You will have to create a Smart Home Groups and add your devices there..

Create Smart Home Groups

Grouping your devices make them easier to manage and control. With Smart Home Groups you can give a simple instruction and Alexa will carry it out on all devices. Create Smart Home Groups by doing the following:

1. Start the Alexa app.
2. Go to the menu and select "**Add Device**"
3. Select the type of Smart home devices and groups you want to connect.
4. Choose the brand of the device and adhere to the subsequent follow-up instructions that will pop up.
5. Click on "**Done**".

Editing a Smart Home Group

You can edit a Smart Home Group after you have created it. You can edit it to add a new device or to remove a device. Editing could also involve changing a few Settings or deleting the Smart Home Group entirely. Here's how you do it.

1. Launch the Alexa app
2. Go to the "**Smart Home Menu**"
3. Choose "**Groups**"
4. Then edit the group as you wish.

Deleting a Smart Home Group

Here's how to delete a Smart Home Group

1. Start the Alexa app
2. Go to the "**Smart Home Menu**"
3. Select "**Groups**"
4. Choose "**Edit Your Group**"
5. Then Delete

Setting Up and Managing Smart Thermostats

With Alexa, you can control room temperature in your home with your voice. This feature is super cool and takes away all the stress in keeping your home warm. This subheading walks you through the process of setting up your Nest Smart Home thermostat. Here's how to go about it.

Before then, know that the Echo Show 8 and the Nest Thermostat make a good combination. You can adjust your room temperature from your Echo Show 8 when it's hooked up with the Best Thermostat. Here is how to add the Nest Thermostat to your Echo Show 8.

1. Start the Alexa app
2. Select the option "**Smart Home**" from the options on the menu.

3. Scroll through the list. Stop only when you get to "**Get More Smart Home Skills**".
4. Select the arrow
5. Choose "**Enable Skill**"
6. Go back to your Nest Account and accept

As you have done this, you have this; you have successfully connected your Echo Show 8 to your Nest Smart Home Thermostat. You can begin giving it instructions.

The same process applied when you want to link your Echo Show 8 with other thermostats like the Honeywell thermostat. It is very easy to carry out and the results are amazing.

CHAPTER 6

Drop Ins And Maintaining Privacy

The Echo Show 8 also has the intercom feature which is also known as Drop In. The feature allows you to get in touch and reach others via video call. The Drop In calls are connected automatically, which means that you don't have to pick the call. Once a Drop In is made, it activates on the other end.

The fact that it connects immediately is the upside and the downside of the Drop In feature. The upside is that all calls come in automatically, while the downside is that your privacy is jeopardy. This is because once the call comes in, the person on the other end will see everything within the range of the device.

You could be Dropped In on without any prior notice and caught unawares.

The Drop In feature can be used for fun, communication and even learning. The scenarios in which this Drop In feature comes in helpful are many. You can use the feature to monitor little children as they sleep or whenever they are alone in a room. You can also use it to keep an eye on your home whenever you are away from home.

In this chapter, we focus on how to set up this feature and enjoy it fully without putting your privacy at risk. Other settings with regards to listening to the content you want and keeping off unwholesome content from your Echo Show Device are discussed as well.

Extending Drop-in beyond Your Household

You can extend this feature beyond the Echo devices in your home; you may decide to add an Echo Device at your office so you could Drop In there as well. Here's what you need to do:

1. Launch the Alexa app
2. Go to Menu
3. Go to the "**Conversations**" option and select it
4. Choose "**Contacts**"
5. Choose the contact you want to Drop-In on
6. Toggle it on

Viewing Approved Drop-in Contacts

The good news about Drop-Ins is that only approved contacts can Drop-In on you. Thus nobody will Drop-In on you if without you approving their contact. Here is how to know which of your contacts are approved to drop-in.

1. Launch the messaging app on the home screen.
2. Choose "**Contacts**"
3. Select yourself, you can then view all the contacts you have approved to Drop-In on you

How to Clear your Alexa History via Alexa App

As you make use of your Echo Show 8, voice recordings and other data will be sent to Amazon cloud storage. You can access those files using the Alexa app. If you wish to maintain a high level of privacy, you can delete these recordings. Here's how to do it:

1. Launch the Alexa app
2. Follow this path **Setting** > **Alexa Privacy** > **Review Voice History**
3. You will be presented with a collection of your recordings
4. Browse through the recordings and click "**Delete Voice Recordings**"

Delete Alexa History via PC

You can also clear your voice recording with any internet-enabled computer. To delete Alexa history via PC, follow these steps:

1. Launch your web browser and visit https://www.amazon.com
2. Log in to your Amazon account
3. Select the option "**Accounts and Lists**"

4. Choose **"Content and Devices"**
5. Select "**Your Devices**", then select "**Echo Show 8**"
6. Select "**Manage Your Recordings**"
7. Select "**Delete**"

Using Your Voice to delete Alexa conversations

You can delete the voice conversations you have recorded by Alexa by asking Alexa to delete them. Before that, you will have to enable the Deletion by Voice feature. Here is how to do it;

1. Launch the Alexa app
2. Go to "**Settings**"
3. Choose your Alexa account
4. Choose "**Alexa Privacy**"
5. Select "**Review Voice History**"

6. Then turn on the "**Enable Deletion by Voice**" button.

Having done this, you can speak to Alexa and ask that your recordings be deleted. For example, you can say, "Alexa, delete everything I said today" or "Alexa, delete everything I said this month".

How to set up Auto-Delete for your Alexa Recordings

Your device can be set to delete recordings of your voice automatically. You can set it to automatically delete after a while in a cycle. Here is what you need to do;

1. Launch the Alexa app.
2. Go to "**Settings**"
3. Go to the "**Manage Your Alexa Data**" option

4. Select "**Manage Your Voice Recordings**"
5. Toggle on the "**Automatically Delete Recordings**" tab, and set the timing. You can set recordings to be deleted after between 3 months or even 18 months.

Setup Parental Controls with FreeTime

This feature helps keep your children safe as they make use of your Echo Show Device. With this feature, you can set limits to how your child makes use of your device. With this feature, you do not have to follow your children to keep an eye on what they are using the device for. With this, you can set what type of content they get to see and relax.

FreeTime is more than just a limiting feature for children. It is a world of educational, entertaining content that children will enjoy. To use this feature, you must enable it from the Alexa app. Afterward, go to the "Settings option" and then select the Parent dashboard to begin.

Follow these steps to enable FreeTime:

1. Launch the Alexa app
2. Tap on the three lines sign on the top left corner
3. Choose "**Settings**" and then "**Device Settings**"
4. Select the device for which you want to activate FreeTime
5. Choose "**FreeTime**" and enable it.
6. Another page will open, on the new page select "**Setup Amazon FreeTime**"

7. Follow the instructions that appear and click “**Continue**”
8. Choose “**Add Child**” and fill out the blank spaces
9. Select “**Continue**” and review the process
10. Carefully read the privacy policy and accept it.
11. Now return to the “**FreeTime**” menu
12. Select “**Parent Dashboard**” and then find and tap on the name of your child
13. Set the type of content they can access

How to Filter Explicit Music

You can choose to enable an explicit music filter. This filter will filter off any music containing explicit content. With this feature on, only songs your children can listen to will be played by your Echo Show 8.

To turn on this feature:

1. Select "**Settings**" from the main menu.
2. Select "**Music**" then tap on "**Explicit Filter**".
3. Turn it on.

CHAPTER 7

Making Phone calls and Messaging with Alexa

You can make phone calls and send messages with your devices via Alexa. This is possible with the Alexa app on android.

Sending an SMS with Alexa

You can use Alexa to send a text message on your smartphone, especially if it is an android. It is easy to set up;

1. Start the Alexa app
2. Open the "**Conversations**" tab
3. Choose the "**Go To My Profile**" option
4. If you do not see the above option, create your profile. You can create

your profile by selecting the contacts icon.

5. Choose "**My Profile**"
6. Permit Alexa to send messages.

You can now ask Alexa to send messages like this:

"Alexa, send an SMS."

"Alexa, send a text message."

"Alexa, send an SMS to [mention contact]."

"Alexa, send a text message to [mention contact]."

How to Use Alexa in Making Phone Calls

It is also possible to make calls to your contacts on their phones from your Echo Show 8 device. The recipients will receive the call from the phone number tied to your Alexa account.

To call a person who is a contact, say "Alexa, call [mention contact]". Alexa will dial the contact's number. To end a call, simply say "Alexa Hang up".

When you wish to specify which number to call (home or office), for contacts with multiple numbers, you can say for example "Alexa call John work".

You can also call out a number for Alexa to call, for example, "Alexa call 1-8-0-0-8-3-2-6-7-6-3-1"

One amazing feature of the Echo Show is that when you call a number tied to another Echo Show device, it switches to a video call by itself. If you do not want a video call, just say "Video off". You can switch off the video by using the onscreen video button.

Blocking Numbers from Calling You

You can prevent certain numbers from reaching. You can, however, block only numbers that are on your contact lists. Here is how;

1. Go to the "**Calling and Messaging**" tab
2. Select the "**Contacts**" icon
3. Open the menu with three lines
4. Select "**Block Contacts**"
5. Select the contacts you wish to block.

How to Schedule "Do Not Disturb Mode."

The Do Not Disturb mode prevents notifications, Drop Ins, alerts and even calls for as long as it is activated. It is a helpful feature especially if you wish to concentrate or enjoy a good night's sleep.

You can set the feature to activate and deactivate at certain periods. Follow the steps outlined:

1. First, visit the "**Settings**" menu
2. Select "**Device Settings**"
3. Choose your device
4. Select "**Do Not Disturb**" and switch it on
5. Switch on "**Scheduled**"
6. Set the times you wish the feature to be activated and deactivated.

CHAPTER 8

Shopping With Alexa

You can make purchases with your Echo Show 8. You have millions of products from Amazon to choose from, and you can buy anyone by simply speaking.

Shopping on Alexa

By default, shopping by voice is activated on your device. Once you register your Echo Show 8, you are good to go.

Assuming you wish to purchase soda;

1. Say "Alexa, order 6 cans of soda". You may be specific and mention the brand you want.
2. Alexa will listen and respond with available options, stating the price and other details.

3. If you want a particular option, say “Yes”. The order will be made.

To turn off the Voice Purchases feature follow this path in the Alexa App

Go to the **Menu** > **Settings** > **Alexa account** > Choose **Voice Purchasing** and then disable the feature

With Voice Purchasing turned off, you cannot make purchases again but you can ask Alexa to track your orders and give you product information.

Setting Up Passwords for Voice Purchases

Set up passwords for Voice Purchases to provide an extra layer of security for you. This helps to prevent unauthorized purchases. With the feature in place,

Alexa will request for a 4 digit pin before purchases are completed. Here's how to set Voice Code.

1. Go to the "**Voice Purchasing**" option
2. Toggle on "**Voice Code**"
3. Key in a 4 digit code on the screen
4. Once activated, you'll have to say the 4 digits before the purchase is completed.

Setting Voice Code Confirmation for Recognized Speakers

With this feature, you and other recognized users do not need to say their codes all the time. It works by setting your voice as a recognized voice and stating your 4 digits once. To have this done, turn the Recognized Voice feature on, you will have to state your 4 digit PIN once.

CHAPTER 9

Using IFTTT with Alexa

IFTTT (which means If This Then That) is a special service. It allows your Echo Show 8 to connect with other IFTTT compatible smart home devices. IFTTT applets are commonly known as Recipes. When hooked up, these recipes allow your Echo Show 8 to work with these devices and do these awesome things. With your Alexa device well synced, you can speak to Alexa to trigger certain events. You can switch on lights, smart devices and so on.

There are hundreds of recipes on the IFTTT site. To know the best recipes, check out the reviews and scores. Here's how to link your Echo Show Device to the IFTTT service.

1. Visit IFTTT.com
2. Tap on "**Sign In**"
3. Several channels on the page, select "**Amazon Alexa**"
4. Put in your Amazon details and click "**Sign In**"
5. Browse through the recipes available.
6. Add recipes that you believe will be helpful to you. Add the recipes by clicking "**Add**".
7. Your Alexa device can now sync with IFTTT compatible devices.

Setting an Alarm from home or Away from Home

Setting an alarm is as easy as saying "Alexa, set an alarm for 5:30 am" and the alarm is set. However, how do you set the alarms when you are away from home? You do it like this;

1. Go to "**Reminders and Alarms**" on the Alexa app on your smartphone.
2. Choose "**Alarms**"
3. Select "**Add Alarms**"
4. Put in the time you want the alarm to go off
5. Choose the alarm tone.

How to Set Alexa Voice Reminders

You can create a reminder by asking Alexa to remind you of anything. Just start by saying "**Alexa, create a new reminder**".

You can, however, create a specific reminder at once, for example, you can say "Alexa, remind me to call Jane at 7:45

am". You can also create reoccurring reminders by voice. For example, "Alexa, remind me to prepare for the gym every morning at 6:00 am".

How to cancel reminders

It is easy to cancel reminders by voice

1. Ask Alexa to show you your active reminders by saying, "**Alexa, show me my reminders**".
2. A numbered list of upcoming reminders will appear.
3. Cancel any reminder you wish by saying for example, "**Alexa cancel number 4 or 6 (or any other number)**".
4. Alexa will respond by confirming that the reminder has been canceled.

Setting a Timer You can set several labeled timers. If you are carrying out two separate tasks that need timing simultaneously, you can set two different timers that will run concurrently. You just Alexa to do it by saying something like "Alexa, an exercise timer for 2 minutes" and "Alexa set a skin treatment timer for 5 minutes".

Both timers will be created and kept at the Timers section of the app where you can adjust it as you wish.

Creating To-do lists

To-Do lists and shopping lists are very easy to create with the Alexa app.

1. Launch the Alexa app

2. Click on the **Hamburger icon**
3. Choose the option for "**Lists**"
4. When you complete a task, swipe it to the right.

You can even switch items between your shopping list and your To-Do lists.

Changing Alexa's Wake Word

Alexa is the personal assistant that powers your Echo show 8. It is why you address your commands to it by saying "Alexa". You can, however, change the name if you wish. This is how you do it.

1. Open the Amazon Alexa app
2. Select the three-line menu
3. Go to "**Settings**"
4. Choose "**Device Settings**"
5. Choose the device you wish to further personalize

6. Select “**Wake word**”
7. Choose the word you wish to change to from an available list of words.

How to Sync your calendar

You can have Alexa go through your calendar and read your upcoming appointments to you. By doing that, you will not need to check your schedules all the time on your phone. Alexa can be synced with Apple Calendar, Google calendar, and Microsoft calendar.

1. Start the Alexa app
2. Choose the “**Menu**” icon
3. Go to “**Settings**”
4. Select “**Calendar & Email**”
5. Then “**Add Account**”
6. Select the calendar service you wish to sync to your Echo device

7. Log in with your credentials for that calendar service
8. Select “**Allow**” when you are presented with the privileges you are granting the calendar service.
9. Set the calendar as you wish.

After you have synced your Echo Show 8 with your calendar service, you can add events or check your schedule by simply speaking to Alexa. For instance, you can ask Alexa to create a new event by saying "Add wedding ceremony to my calendar for 10:00 a.m tomorrow" or you can ask "Alexa, what is on my calendar for this week?"

Troubleshooting

Device Having Difficulty Connecting via Bluetooth

1. Ensure that the device you wish to connect to your Echo Show 8 supports Bluetooth. Alexa devices use the Advanced Audio Distribution Profile (A2DP SNK) and the Audio/Video Remote Control Profile (AVRCP) for Bluetooth connectivity.
2. Charge the battery of your Bluetooth device or put new batteries.
3. Bring your Bluetooth device closer to the Echo Show 8
4. Move both devices from objects of interference such as microwave ovens, and other devices.

5. Try pairing both devices again.

Device Screen Having Bars on the Screen

The bars appearing on the screen could be as a result of the screen being too bright. You can solve this by lowering the screen's brightness. Turning off Auto-Brightness will also work

Unresponsive Screen

Tiny infrared lights that surround the screen help the touchscreen function. When dust and other particles block the infrared light, the screen may become insensitive to touch. Clean the screen with a soft cloth to remove dust and particles.

Devices like printers and microwave ovens may create interference that can make your screen unresponsive. Move your device away and reboot your Echo Show 8.

Device Not Charging

Several reasons could be why the device is not charging.

1. Check the adapter for faults. Replace the adapter to see if the fault is from the adapter.
2. Check that the charging cord is in good shape and firmly connected.

Device Not Connecting to Wi-Fi

When the Wi-Fi is switched on but the Echo Show device is not connected to it, several factors may be at play.

1. Check the router to ensure it is working. Restart the router.

2. Check that you have entered the correct password.
3. Restart your Echo Show Device.

Resetting Your Echo Device

Several factors may warrant that you reset your device. You may be giving it out as a gift, or you are about to sell it off. Resetting it is a way to restore all settings to how they were from the factory and remove all personal data.

You can reset the device from the Alexa app.

1. Launch the Alexa app on your smartphone or tablet.
2. Tap on the "Devices" button.
3. Select Echo and Alexa.
4. Choose the device you wish to reset.

5. Find where it is written "Device Registered To" and select "Deregister".
6. Confirm that you want to reset the device by selecting "Deregister" in the next window.
7. Your device has been reset.

Made in the USA
Middletown, DE
03 March 2020

85729664R00060